KETO SLOV
COOKBUUK

THE BEST HIGH-FAT, LOW CARB SLOW COOKER RECIPES

—
5

Introduction

A diet that results in the production of ketone bodies by the liver is called a ketogenic diet; it causes your system to use fat instead of carbohydrates for energy. Limit your carbohydrate intake to a low level, causing some reactions. However, it is not a high protein diet. It involves moderate protein, low carbohydrate intake, and high fat intake.

You're probably wondering: The aim of a diet is to lose weight and not to gain more. How does that happen if I'm replacing carbs with fat? It is quite simple, really. When the levels of carbs in your body start to dwindle, your body goes into a metabolic state. This metabolic state is referred to as ketosis. The ketosis state is one in which the body burns fat much more rapidly to convert it into energy. The fat is not only turned to energy but is also turned into ketones. Ketones located in the liver also boost energy. In summary, Keto changes your body's mode of operation. Rather than converting your carbohydrates into energy, the fats you want to rid your body of are converted and burned off instead. The end result of a Keto diet is burned fat, boosted energy, reduced insulin levels, and reduced blood sugar.

Regardless of your lifestyle, everyone benefits from the keto diet in the following ways:

Weight Loss

Far more important than the visual aspect of excess weight is its negative influence on your body. Too much weight affects the efficiency of your body's blood flow, which in turn also affects how much oxygen your heart is able to pump to every part of your system. Too much weight also means that there are layers of fat covering your internal organs, which prevent them from working efficiently. It makes it hard to walk because it puts great pressure on your joints and makes it very difficult to complete even regular daily tasks. A healthy weight allows your body to move freely and your entire internal system to work at its optimal levels.

Cognitive Focus

In order for your brain to function at its best, it needs to have balanced levels of all nutrients and molecules, because a balance allows it to focus on other things, such as working, studying, or creativity. If you eat carbs, the sudden insulin spike that comes with them will force your brain to stop whatever it was doing and to turn its focus on the correct breakdown of glucose molecules. This is why people often feel sleepy and with a foggy mind after high-carb meals. The keto diet keeps the balance strong so that your brain does not have to deal with any sudden surprises.

Blood Sugar Control

If you already have diabetes or are prone to it, then controlling your blood sugar is obviously of the utmost importance. However, even if you are not battling a type of diabetes at the moment, that doesn't mean that you are not in danger of developing it in the future. Most people forget that insulin is a finite resource in your body. You are given a certain amount of it, and it is gradually used up throughout your life. The more often you eat carbs, the more often your body needs to use insulin to break down the glucose, and when it reaches critically low levels of this finite resource, diabetes is formed.

Lower Cholesterol and Blood Pressure

Cholesterol and triglyceride levels maintain or ruin your arterial health. If your arteries are clogged up with cholesterol, they cannot efficiently transfer blood through your system, which in some cases even results in heart attacks. The keto diet keeps all of these levels at an optimal level so that they do not interfere with your body's normal functioning.

Slow Cookers

Slow cookers are not new appliances in the culinary world. They have been around for decades; you might even have fond memories from your childhood of your parents serving your favorite dinner out of one. Slow cookers are very versatile because the cooking environment works the same no matter the cuisine. Knowing what slow cookers can and can't do is important for planning your meals, especially for a diet like keto.

In this chapter, you will learn slow-cooker basics such as which kind is best for your needs, how to ensure your recipes turn out great, and how to convert your traditional family favorites to work for you. Taking the mystery out of the slow cooker should give you the confidence to create spectacular keto meals as often as you want in order to reach your goals while eating well.

Some of the reasons to use a slow cooker include:

Enhances flavor: Cooking ingredients over several hours with spices, herbs, and other seasonings creates vegetables and proteins that burst with delicious flavors. This slow process allows the flavors to mellow and deepen for an enhanced eating experience.

Saves time: Cooking at home takes a great deal of time: prepping, sautéing, stirring, turning the heat up and down, and watching the meal so that it does not over- or undercook. If you're unable to invest the time, you might find yourself reaching for convenience foods instead of healthy choices. Slow cookers allow you to do other activities while the meal cooks. You can put your ingredients in the slow cooker in the morning and come home to a perfectly cooked meal.

Convenient: Besides the time-saving aspect, using a slow cooker can free up the stove and oven for other dishes. This can be very convenient for large holiday meals or when you want to serve a side dish and entrée as well as a delectable dessert. Clean up is simple when you use the slow cooker for messy meals because most inserts are nonstick or are easily cleaned with a little soapy water, and each meal is prepared in either just the machine or using one additional vessel to sauté ingredients. There is no wide assortment of pots, pans, and baking dishes to contend with at the end of the day.

Low heat production: If you have ever cooked dinner on a scorching summer afternoon, you will appreciate the low amount of heat produced by a slow cooker. Even after eight hours of operation, slow cookers do not heat up your kitchen, and you will not be sweating over the hot stovetop. Slow cookers use about a third of the energy of conventional cooking methods, just a little more energy than a traditional light bulb.

Supports healthy eating: Cooking your food at high heat can reduce the nutrition profile of your foods, breaking down and removing the majority of vitamins, minerals, and antioxidants while producing unhealthy chemical compounds that can contribute to disease. Low-heat cooking retains all the goodness that you want for your diet.

Saves Money: Slow cookers save you money because of the low amount of electricity they use and because the best ingredients for slow cooking are the less expensive cuts of beef and heartier inexpensive vegetables. Tougher cuts of meat—brisket, chuck, shanks—break down beautifully to fork-tender goodness. Another cost-saving benefit is that most 6-quart slow cookers will produce enough of a recipe to stretch your meals over at least two days. Leftovers are one of the best methods for saving money.

Why Choose the Keto Diet, Benefits, and Risk

The word keto is short for ketogenic. The Ketogenic diet focuses on consuming very low amounts of carbohydrates, high levels of fat, and adequate levels of protein. In simple terms, with the Keto diet, you replace carbohydrates with fat. In case you haven't figured this out, carbohydrates are known as carbs, for short.

You all know that our body needs energy for its functioning, and the energy sources come from carbohydrates, proteins, and fats. Owing to years of conditioning that a low-fat carbohydrate-rich diet is essential for good health, we have become used to depending on glucose (from carbohydrates) to get most of the energy that our body needs. Only when the amount of glucose available for energy generation decreases does our body begin to break down fat for drawing energy to power our cells and organs. This is the express purpose of a ketogenic diet.

The primary aim of a ketogenic diet (called only as of the keto diet) is to convert your body into a fat-burning machine. Such a diet is loaded with benefits and is highly recommended by nutritional experts for the following results:

• Natural appetite control

- Increased mental clarity

- Lowered levels of inflammation in the body system

- Improved stability in blood sugar levels

- Elimination or lower risk of heartburn

- Using natural stored body fat as the fuel source

- Weight loss

The effects listed are just some of the numerous impacts that take place when a person embarks on a ketogenic diet and makes it a point to stick to it. A ketogenic diet consists of meals with low carbohydrates, moderate proteins, and high-fat content. The mechanism works like this: when we drastically reduce the intake of carbohydrates, our body is compelled to convert fat for releasing energy. This process of converting fats instead of carbohydrates to release energy is called Ketosis.

BENEFITS KETOGENIC DIET

Reduction of risk of heart disease

Triglycerides, fat molecules in your body, have close links with heart disease. They are directly proportional as the more the number of triglycerides, the higher your chances of suffering from heart disease. You can reduce the number of free triglycerides in your body by reducing the number of carbohydrates, as is in the keto diets.

Reduces chances of having high blood pressure

Weight loss and blood pressure have a close connection; thus, since you are losing weight while on the keto diet, it will affect your blood pressure.

Fights type 2 diabetes

Type two diabetes develops as a result of insulin resistance. This is a result of having huge amounts of glucose in your system, with the keto diet this is not a possibility due to the low carbohydrate intake.

Increases the production of HDL

High-density lipoprotein is referred to as good cholesterol. It is responsible for caring calories to your liver, thus it can be reused. High fat and low-carbohydrate diets increase the production of HDL in your body, which also reduces your chances of getting a heart disease. Low-density lipoprotein is referred to as bad cholesterol.

Suppresses your appctite

It is a strange but true effect of the keto diet. It was thought that this was a result of the production of ketones, but this was proven wrong as a study taken between people on a regular balanced diet and some on the keto diet, and their appetites were generally the same. It, however, helps to suppress appetite as it is it has a higher fat content than many other diets. Food stays in the stomach for longer as fat and is digested slowly, thus provides a sense of fullness. On top of that, proteins promote the secretion cholecystokinin, which is a hormone that aids in regulating appetite. It is also believed that the ketogenic diet helps to suppress your appetite by continuous blunting of appetite. There is increased appetite in the initial stages of the diet, which decreases over time.

Changes in cholesterol levels

This is kind of on the fence between good and bad. This is because the ketogenic diet involves a high fat intake, which makes people wonder about the effect on blood lipids and its potential to increase chances of heart disease and strokes, among others. Several major components play a lead role in determining this, which is: LDL, HDL, and blood triglyceride levels. Heart disease correlates with high levels of LDL and cholesterol. On the other hand, high levels of HDL are seen as protection from diseases caused by cholesterol levels. The impacts of the diet on cholesterol are not properly known. Some research has shown that there is no change in cholesterol levels while others have said that there is change. If you stay in deep ketosis for a very long period of time, your blood lipids will increase, but you will have to go through some negative effects of the ketogenic diet, which will be corrected when the diet is over. If a person does not remain following the diet strictly for ten years, he/she will not experience any cholesterol problems. It is difficult to differentiate the difference between diet and weight loss in general. The effect of the ketogenic diet on cholesterol has been boiled down to if you lose fat on the ketogenic diet, then your cholesterol levels will go down, and if you don't lose fat, then your cholesterol levels will go up. Strangely, women have a larger cholesterol level addition than men, while both are on a diet. As there is no absolute conclusion on the effect of the ketogenic diet on cholesterol, you are advised to have your blood lipid levels constantly checked for any bad effects. Blood lipid levels should be checked before starting the diet and about eight weeks after starting. If repeated results show a worsening of lipid levels, then you should abandon the diet or substitute saturated fats with unsaturated fats.

Risk of a Ketogenic Diet

Low energy levels

When available, the body prefers to use carbohydrates for fuel as they burn more effectively than fats. General drop-in energy level is a concern raised by many dieters due to the lack of carbohydrates. Studies have shown that it causes orthostatic hypotension, which causes lightheadedness. It has come to be known that these effects can be avoided by providing enough supplemental nutrients like sodium. Many of the symptoms can be prevented by providing 5 grams of sodium per day. Most times, fatigue disappears after a few weeks or even days, if fatigue doesn't disappear, then you should add a small number of carbohydrates to the diet as long as ketosis is maintained. The diet is not recommended when doing high-intensity workouts, weight training, or high-intensity aerobic exercise as carbohydrates are an absolute requirement but are okay for low-intensity exercise.

Effects on the brain

It causes increased use of ketones by the brain. The increased use of ketones, among other reasons, result in the treating of childhood epilepsy. As a result of the changes that occur, the concern over the side effects, including permanent brain damage and short-term memory loss, has been raised. The origin of these concerns is difficult to understand. The brain is powered by ketones in the absence of glucose. Ketones are normal energy sources and not toxic as the brain creates enzymes during fetal growth that helps us use them. Epileptic children, though not the perfect examples, show some insight into the effects of the diet on the brain in the long term. There is no negative effect in terms of cognitive function. There is no assurance that the diet cannot have long-term dietary effects, but no information proves that there are any negative effects. Some people feel they can concentrate more when on the ketogenic diet, while others feel nothing but fatigue. This is as a result of differences in individual physiology. There are very few studies that vaguely address the point on short-term memory loss. This wore off with the continuation of the study.

Kidney stones and kidney damage

The high protein nature of the ketogenic diet raises the alarms of individuals who are concerned with potential kidney damage. There is very little information that points to any negative effects of the diet on kidney function or the development of kidney stones. There is a low incidence of small kidney stones in epileptic children, this may be a result of the state of deliberate dehydration that the children are put at instead of the ketosis state itself. Some short-term research shows no change in kidney function or increased incidents of kidney stones either after they are off the diet or after six months on a diet. There is no long-term data on the effects of ketosis on kidney function; thus, no complete conclusions can be made. People with preexisting kidney issues are the only ones who get problems from high protein intake. From an unscientific point of view, one would expect increased incidents of this to happen to athletes who consume very high-protein diets, but it has not happened. This suggests that high protein intake, under normal conditions, is not harmful to the kidneys. To limit the possibility of kidney stones, it is advised to drink a lot of water to maintain hydration. For people who are predisposed to kidney stones should have their kidney function should be monitored to ensure that no complications arise if they decide to follow through with the diet.

Constipation

A common side effect of the diet is reduced bowel movements and constipation. This arises from two different causes: lack of fiber and gastrointestinal absorption of foods. First, the lack of carbs in the diet means that unless supplements are taken, fiber intake is low. Fiber is very important to our systems. High fiber intake can prevent some health conditions, including heart disease and some forms of cancer. Use some type of sugar-free fiber supplement to prevent any health problems and help you maintain regular bowel movements. The diet also reduces the volume of stool due to enhanced absorption and digestion of food; thus, fewer waste products are generated.

Fat regain

Dieting, in general, has very low long-term success rates. There are some effects of getting out of a ketogenic diet, like the regain of fat lost through calorific restriction alone. This is true for any diet based on calorific restriction. It is expected for weight to be regained after carb reintroduction. For people who use the weighing scale to measure their success they may completely shun carbs as they think it is the main reason for the weight regain. You should understand that most of the initial weight gain is water and glycogen.

Immune system

There is a large variety in the immune system response to ketogenic diets on different people. There has been some repost on reduction on some ailments such as allergies and increased minor sickness susceptibility.

Optic neuropathy

This is optic nerve dysfunction. It has appeared in a few cases, but it is still existence. It was linked to the people not getting adequate amounts of calcium or vitamin supplements for about a year. All the cases were corrected by supplementation of adequate vitamin B, especially thiamine.

How to Use the Slow Cooker, Tips and Tricks

Slow cookers have changed a lot over the years. These days you can purchase models that range from very simple models all the way to ones that look like they should be on a space station. When buying the right model for your needs, you have to consider what you are cooking, how many portions, and if you will be home during the cooking process. All these factors are important when deciding on the size, shape, and features of your slow cooker.

Size and Shape

Slow cookers come in a multitude of sizes and shapes, so it is important to consider your needs and what will work best for the type of food prepared on the keto diet. There are models that range from ½-quart to large 8-quart models and everything in-between.

The small slow cookers (½-quart to 2-quart) are usually used for dips or sauces, as well as recipes designed for one person. Medium-sized slow cookers (3-quart to 4-quart) are great for baking or for meals that create food for two to three people. The slow cooker recommended for most of the recipes in this book is the 5-quart to 6-quart model because it is perfect for the large cuts of meat on the keto diet and can prepare food for four people, including leftovers. The enormous 7-quart to 8-quart appliance is meant for very large meals. If you have money in your budget, owning both a 3-quart and 6-quart model would be the best of both worlds.

When it comes to shapes, you will have to decide between round, oval, and rectangular. Round slow cookers are fine for stews and chili but do not work well for large pieces of meat. These should probably not be your choice. Oval and rectangular slow cookers both allow for the ingredients you will use regularly that are large, like roasts, ribs, and chops, and have the added advantage of fitting loaf pans, ramekins, and casserole dishes, as well. Some desserts and breads are best cooked in another container placed in the slow cooker, and you will see several recipes in this book that use that technique.

Features

Now that you know the size and shape of the recommended slow cooker, it is time to consider what you want this appliance to do for you. Depending on your budget, at a minimum you want a slow cooker with temperature controls that cover warm, low, and high, as well as a removable insert. These are the primary features of the bare-bones models that will get the job done. However, if you want to truly experience a set-it-and-forget-it appliance that creates the best meals possible in this cooking environment, you might want to consider the following features:

Digital programmable controls: You can program temperature, when the slow cooker starts, how long it cooks, and when the slow cooker switches to warm.

Glass lid: These are heavier and allow you to look into the slow cooker without removing them, so there is little heat loss. Opt for a lid with clamps, and you can transport your cooked meal easily to parties and gatherings if needed.

Temperature probe: Once you have a slow cooker with this feature, you will wonder how you cooked previously without it. The temperature probe allows you to cook your meat, poultry, and egg dishes to an exact temperature and then switches to warm when completed.

Precooking feature: Some models have a precooking feature that allows you to brown your meat and poultry right in the insert. You will still have to take the time to do this step, but you won't have a skillet to clean afterward.

TIPS FOR SLOW-COOKING SUCCESS

Slow cookers are simple to use, but you can increase your success with a few tips and techniques. In the following list, some tips are suggestions, and some should be considered more seriously for safety or health reasons. The intent is to provide the best information possible so that your meals are delicious and easy.

Always

Read the user manual and any other literature. You will find an assortment of instructions included in the slow-cooker box, so take the time to sit down and read everything completely before using a new device. You might think you know how everything works, but each model is a little different, and it is best to be informed about all of the things your slow cooker can do.

Grease the insert of the slow cooker before cooking. Cleaning a slow cooker insert can be a challenge, so grease the insert, even for soups and stews. You don't want to scrub the insert with abrasive brushes or scraping bits of cooked-on food off, because you will wreck its nonstick surface.

Add dairy and herbs at the end of the cooking process. As stated elsewhere in this book, dairy and fresh herbs do not hold up well during long cooking times. Dairy splits and creates a grainy, unpleasant texture, and herbs lose their flavor, color, and texture. Always add these ingredients at the end.

Always cut your ingredients into similar-sized pieces. Slow cookers are not meant to be used for staggered cooking recipes such as stir-fries, where the more delicate ingredients are added last to avoid overcooking. Evenly sized pieces mean your ingredients will be ready at the same time, and your meals will be cooked evenly.

Adjust your seasonings. Slow cookers can have an unexpected effect on herbs and spices so it is important to taste and adjust at the end of the process. Some spices, such as curry or cayenne, can get more intense, while the long cooking time can reduce the impact of dried herbs. It is best to hold off on too much salt until the very end as well, because it will get stronger.

Never

Use frozen meats or poultry. The ingredients in slow cookers need to reach 140°F within 4 hours for food safety, so large cuts of meat or poultry should be fully thawed. You can add small frozen items like meatballs to a slow cooker because these can come to temperature within this time range.

Place your insert right from the refrigerator into the slow cooker. When you remove your previously prepared meal from the refrigerator, let the insert sit out at room temperature for 30 minutes or so to avoid cracking it with extreme temperature changes. Also, never remove the hot insert from your slow cooker and place it on a cold surface.

Resume cooking after a power outage of over two hours. Power outages can happen in any season, and for food-safety reasons, you have to err on the side of caution. If an outage lasts for more than two hours, especially during the first few hours of the cooking time, you need to discard the food because the amount of time spent in the food danger zone ($40\,°F$ to $140\,°F$) will have been too long. If the outage is less than two hours and it occurs after your food has been cooking for at least four hours, then you can resume cooking until the end of the original time or transfer the food to a pot or casserole dish and finish it on the stove or in the oven. When in doubt, throw the food out.

Use the recommended cooking times in high altitudes. As with most other cooking methods, slow cookers need more cooking time if you live above an altitude of 3,000 feet. The liquid in the slow cooker will simmer at a lower temperature, so high-heat settings are recommended, or if you can program the slow cooker, then set it to maintain the food at $200\,°F$ or higher. You can also use a temperature probe set to $165\,°F$ internal temperature if your slow cooker has this feature.

Breakfast

Mexican Breakfast Casserole

Preparation Time: 15 minutes

Cooking Time: 2 hours and 30 minutes

Servings: 10

Ingredients:

- Pork Sausage Roll - 12 ounces (I prefer Jones Dairy)

- Garlic powder - ½ teaspoon

- Coriander – ½ teaspoon

- Cumin - 1 teaspoon

- Salsa – 1 cup

- Chili fine powder - 1 teaspoon

- Salt - ¼ teaspoon

- Pepper - ¼ teaspoon

- Eggs - 10

- Milk low fat - 1 cup

- Cheese (Pepper Jack if available) - 1 cup

- Toppings if required: Avocado salsa, sour cream, cilantro – as per preference

Directions:

1. Put a pan on low flame and cook pork sausage until it leaves its pink color.

2. Add all the spices given and let it cool and set for some time.

3. Now take a medium bowl and whisk eggs and milk together.

4. Add the pork to the eggs and stir well so that they get

5. mixed properly.

6.   Take a crock pot and grease its bottom and pour the mixture you prepared.

7.   Cook on high flame for 2 hours and 30 minutes.

8.   You can put seasonal toppings on it according to your taste.

Nutrition:

Fat: 24 g

Saturated fat: 8.5 g

Cholesterol: 231 g

Sodium: 749 mg

Carbohydrates:5.2 g

Protein: 17.9 g

Dietary fiber: 2.6 g

Potassium: 454 mg

Cauliflower Hash Browns Slow Breakfast Casserole

Preparation Time: 15 minutes

Cooking Time: 5-7 hours

Servings: 10

Ingredients:

- Eggs - 12

- Milk - ½ cup

- Dry mustard - ½ teaspoon

- Kosher salt - 1 teaspoon

- Pepper - ½ teaspoon

- Cauliflower, shredded - 1 head

- Additional salt and pepper to season the layers – as required

- Small onion, diced - 1

- Packaged pre-cooked breakfast sausages, sliced – 5 ounces

- Shredded cheddar cheese – 8 ounces

Directions:

1. First of all, grease a 6-quart slow cooker properly with cooking spray.

2. Mix well all the item likes the eggs, milk, dry mustard, salt, and pepper.

3. From the shredded cauliflower, take one-third portion and layer it in the bottom of the slow crock pot. After that, place one-third of the sliced onion on top.

4. Use pepper and salt to season and top it with one-third portion of sausage and cheese.

5. Repeat the same process by maintaining two layers.

6. Pour the eggs mixture over the slow cooker

7. Cook on low for 5-7 hours and wait until eggs set properly, and the top color is browned.

Nutrition:

Calories 87.7

Calories from Fat 49

Total Fat 5.4 g

Cholesterol 1mg

Total Carbohydrates 2.2g

Dietary Fiber 1.2g

Protein 8g

Breakfast Casserole

Preparation Time: 15-20 minutes

Cooking Time: 6 hours

Servings: 8

Ingredients:

- Brown jicama, hashed or brown daikon radish - 4 cups

- Cooked, crumbled, and drained bacon slices - 12 ounces

- Cooked, drained and grounded sausage - 1 pound

- Onion, sweet yellow, chopped - 1

- Diced green bell pepper – 1

- Fresh mushroom, sliced - 1 to ½ cups

- Fresh spinach - 1 to ½ cups

- Shredded cheese - 2 cups (Monterrey Jack preferred)

- Feta cheese, shredded - ½ cup

- Eggs - 1 dozen

- Heavy white cream - 1 cup

- Salt - 1 tablespoon

- Pepper - 1 tablespoon

Directions:

1.   First of all, put a layer of hashed browns in the bottom of the cooker with a low flame.

2.   Then put the layer of bacon and sausage over it.

3.   Put all the spices upon the layer.

4.   Now take a bowl and whisk the eggs, cream, salt, and pepper together.

5.   Pour the mixture of eggs into the cooker.

6.   Cover it and let it cook for 6 hours on high flame or for 12 hours on low flame.

Nutrition:

Calories 443

Carbohydrates8 g

Fat 38 g

Fiber 2 g

Protein18 g

Bacon-Mushroom Breakfast

Preparation Time: 15 minutes

Cooking Time: 1 hour 45 minutes

Servings: 4

Ingredients:

- Bacon large, sliced – 3½ Ounces

- White mushrooms, chopped – 2½ Ounces

- Eggs – 6 Nos.

- Shallots, chopped – 3 Tablespoons

- Bell pepper, chopped - ¾ Cup

- Kale leaves large, shredded – 8 Nos.

- Ghee – 1 Tablespoon.

- Parmesan cheese – 1 Cup

- Avocado and green leaves (Optional)

Directions:

1. Clean the kale leaves, remove the hard stems, and chop into small pieces.

2. In a skillet, cook the bacon till it becomes crispy, and add mushrooms, red pepper, and shallot.

3. Add kale and cut down the flame, and let the kale become tender in the skillet.

4. Now take a medium bowl and beat all eggs, add pepper and salt.

5. In the crock pot, add ghee and let it become hot. Spread the ghee on all sides of the cooker.

6. Put the sautéed vegetable into the base of the cooker.

7. Spread the cheese over the vegetables.

8. Then, add the beaten eggs on top.

9. Just stir it gently.

10. Set the cooker on low heat and cook for about 6 hours.

11. Serve hot with sliced avocado and green leaves.

Nutrition :

Calories 313

Carb 4g

Protein 22.9

Fat 22.2

Potassium 503mg

Magnesium 65mg

Keto Sausage & Egg Casserole

Preparation Time: 15-20 minutes

Cooking Time: 4-5 hours

Servings: 6-8

Ingredients:

- Large Eggs - 12

- Pork sausage links, cooked and sliced – 12 ounces

- Broccoli, finely chopped – 1

- Cheddar Shredded – 1 cup

- Whipping cream - ¾ cup

- Garlic cloves, minced - 2

- Salt – to taste (½ teaspoon)

- Pepper – ½ tablespoon

Directions:

1.   Take a 6quart ceramic slow cooker and grease its interior.

2.   Put one layer of broccoli, half portion of the cheese, and half part of sausage into the ceramic cooker. Repeat the layering and put all the ingredients in the cooker.

3.   Take a large bowl and mix eggs, garlic, whipping cream, pepper, and salt thoroughly.

4.   Transfer the mix over the layered ingredients in the ceramic cooker.

5.   Cover and cooker for about 5 hours.

6.   Make sure the edges are not overcooked.

7.   Check the center and make sure your finger bounces back when touching.

Nutrition:

Calories 484

Fat 38.86 g

Cholesterol 399 mg

Potassium 8 mg

Carbohydrates5.39 g

Dietary Fiber1.18 g

Sodium858 mg

Protein26.13 g

Egg & Mushroom Breakfast

Preparation Time: 15 minutes

Cooking Time: 6 hours

Servings: 4

Ingredients:

- Mushrooms, chopped - 1 cup

- Bacon large - 3

- Eggs - 6

- Chopped shallots - 3 tablespoons

- Bell pepper, red - ½ cup

- Shredded kale leaves - 8 large

- Parmesan cheese, shredded - 1 cup

- Butter or ghee - 1 tablespoon

- Pepper - ¼ spoon

- Salt to taste

- Spinach - for dressing

- Avocado, sliced - for dressing

- Virgin olive oil - for dressing

Directions:

1. Wash, clean, and slice the bacon

2. Wash, clean, and remove the stem of the kale and chop it nicely.

3. Take a pan and cook bacon until it becomes crispy.

4. Add mushroom, pepper, and shallot and continue heating until it becomes soft.

5. Now add kale and switch off the stove and let the kale wilt.

6. Take a small mixing bowl and beat the eggs with pepper and salt.

7. Put on the slow cooker and add some butter.

8.   Grease the inside of the cooker properly with the butter.

9.   Transfer the sautéed vegetables to the cooker.

10.   Spread the cheese over it.

11.   Add the beaten egg on top of the mixture.

12.   Stir well and slow heat for 6 hours.

13.   You may occasionally check the food after 4 hours.

14.   Check with your finger to bounce back.

15.   Serve it with sliced avocado, spread with spinach dressed in olive oil.

Nutrition:

Total carbs 6.1 g

Fiber 2.1 g

Net carbs 4 g

Fat 22.2 g

Protein 22.9 g

Saturated fat 9.8 g

Energy313 kcal

Magnesium 65 mg

Potassium 503 mg

Egg, Spinach, and Ham Breakfast Casserole

Preparation Time: 10 minutes

Cooking Time: 1 hour and 30 minutes

Servings: 6

Ingredients:

- Large eggs - 6

- Salt - ½ teaspoon

- Black pepper - ¼ teaspoon

- Milk - ¼ cup

- Greek yogurt - ½ cup

- Thyme - ½ teaspoon

- Onion powder - ½ teaspoon

- Garlic powder - ½ teaspoon

- Diced mushrooms - ⅓ cup

- Baby spinach (packed) – 1 cup

- Shredded pepper jack cheese – 1 cup

- Ham, diced – 1 cup

Directions:

1.   Mix eggs, salt, pepper, milk, yogurt, thyme, onion powder, garlic powder properly in a bowl.

2.   Add mushrooms, spinach, cheese, ham, and stir.

3.   Now take a 6-quart slow cooker and spray with non-stick cooking spray.

4.   Pour egg mixture into the cooker and put on slow.

5.   Cover and cook on high for 90-120 minutes until eggs are appropriately set.

6.   Slice and serve for breakfast or dinner.

Nutrition:

Calories 155.6

Total Fat 8.7 g

Cholesterol 86.1 mg

Sodium 758.8 mg

Total Carbs 2.5 g

Dietary Fiber 0.3 g

Protein15.6 g

Keto Soup with Miso

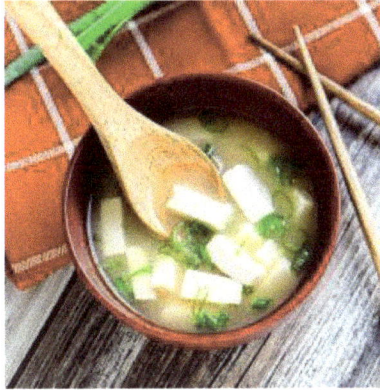

Preparation Time: 15 minutes

Cooking Time: 8 hours

Servings: 4

Ingredients:

- Chopped onion - 1 medium

- Miso, white good quality - 2 tablespoon

- Olive oil - 4 tablespoons

- Garlic, minced - 1 teaspoon

- Broccoli flowerets - 1 cup

- Zucchini, chopped - 1 cup

- Celery stalks, cut into pieces - 2 stalks

- Pumpkin, diced - 1 cup

- Pepper as required

- Salt to taste

Directions:

1. Take a crock pot and put 2 tablespoons olive oil and keep aside.

2. Then take a large skillet, put 2 tablespoons of oil, and heat it.

3. Add onion, garlic, pumpkin, celery to the heating skillet by sprinkling a bit of salt.

4. Sauté for 5 minutes

5. Transfer this mixture to the crock pot and put all other ingredients.

6. Now pour about 4 cups of water and salt to taste.

7. Stir well.

8. Take 3 tablespoons of water and mix the Miso and add to the crock pot.

9. Put it in the slow cooker for about 8 hours.

10.   Serve warm

Nutrition:

Carbohydrate 6 g

Net carbs 4.86 g

Fat 19 g

Fiber 3 g

Protein 12 g

Lunch

Barbecue Beef Stew

Preparation Time: 15 minutes

Cooking Time: 8 hours

Servings: 6

Ingredients:

- 1 jar/homemade (7 oz.) tomato paste

- 1 Balsamic vinegar

- ½ t. black pepper

- 1 t. of each Smoked paprika

- 1 t. of kosher salt

- 1 t. of Garlic powder

- 2 tbsp. sweetener – ex. xylitol

Ingredients for the Stew

- 1 t. kosher salt

- 2 lb. extra-lean stew beef meat/boneless chuck roast

- 1 tbsp. olive oil

- ½ t. black pepper

- 2 tbsp. cold tap water

- 1 tbsp. cornstarch or ½ t. konjac flour

- 14-inch skillet

Directions:

1   Chop the meat into one-inch pieces, and season it with pepper and salt.

2   Combine the barbecue sauce ingredients.

3   Prepare the skillet by adding half of the oil using the med-high setting for three minutes.

4   Add half of the beef and cook for five minutes. Place in the slow cooker.

5   Add the rest of the oil and cook the second half of beef and add it as well.

6   Empty the sauce over the prepared meat and stir. Place the top on the pot and cook for 7 ½ hours on low.

7   Whisk in the cornstarch and water together in a dish until smooth. Empty it into the beef juices. Set the slow cooker on high for 30 minutes.

8   When thickened to your liking, serve, and enjoy.

Nutrition:

445 Calories

10 g Net Carbs

30 g Protein

29 g Fat

Beef Stew with Tomatoes

Preparation Time: 10 minutes

Cooking Time: 8 hours

Servings: 6

Ingredients:

- 1 pkg. (5 lbs.) stew beef

- 2 cans chili-ready diced tomatoes (14.5 oz.) - organic

- 2 t. hot sauce

- 1 c. beef broth

- 1 tbsp. of Chili mix (pre-packaged)

- 1 tbsp. of Worcestershire sauce

- Salt to taste

Directions:

1   Warm up the slow cooker in the high setting.

2   Add the stewing beef, tomatoes, hot sauce, broth, Worcestershire sauce, chili mix, and salt in the slow cooker.

3   Set the timer for six hours. Break the meat apart and continue cooking for another two hours. Sprinkle with a pinch of salt to taste when ready to serve.

Nutrition:

222 Calories

9 g Net Carbs

7 g Fat

27 g Protein

Chicken Stew

Preparation Time: 20 minutes

Cooking Time: 2 hours

Servings: 4

Ingredients:

- 1 pkg. (28 oz.) skinless & deboned chicken thighs

- 2 celery sticks - 1 c. diced

- 1 Onion

- 2 med. carrots – approx.

- 2 c. chicken stock

- ½ t. dried rosemary/1 fresh sprig

- minced cloves of garlic

- Pepper and salt to taste

- ½ t. dried oregano

- ¼ t. dried thyme

- ½ c. heavy cream

- 1 c. fresh spinach

- Xanthan gum as desired (start at ⅛ t.)

- Recommended: 3-quart or larger slow cooker

Directions:

1   Dice the chicken into one-inch chunks.

2   Remove the skin and finely dice the carrots and celery.

3   Add the veggies and chicken to the slow cooker.

4   Pour in the stock, thyme, oregano, rosemary, and garlic in the cooker.

5   Toss in the pepper and salt. Mix in the heavy cream and spinach leaves.

6   Add the xanthan gum to thicken the juices, and simmer another ten minutes.

7   Set the cooker on high for two hours or low setting for four hours.

8   When it's done, enjoy.

Nutrition:

228 Calories

6 g Carbs

11 g Fat

23 g Protein

Hare Stew

Preparation Time: 15 minutes

Cooking Time: 5 hours

Servings: 6

Ingredients:

- ½ lb. uncured organic bacon/smoked pork belly

- 1 whole rabbit/hare (3lb.) cut into pieces

- 2 tbsp. butter

- 2 c. dry white wine

- 1 large Sweet onion

- 1 large Sprig of rosemary

- 1 t. whole peppercorn

- 2 bay leaves

- 2 tbsp. Celtic sea salt

Directions:

1   Cut the pork belly into one-inch bites.

2   Place them in a heated skillet along with the butter.

3   Thinly slice the onion and toss it in.

4   Continue cooking slowly for approximately five minutes, and remove the onion (leaving the grease in the skillet).

5   Arrange the prepared meat bites in the pan and continue cooking using the high setting until browned.

6   Pour in the wine and let it simmer two more minutes.

7   Add all the fixings into the slow cooker.

8   Shake in the rosemary, salt, bay leaves, and peppercorn.

9   Select the low setting for five hours. When done, serve, and enjoy.

Nutrition:

517 Calories

36 g Protein

2 g Net Carbs

32 Fat

Dinner

Pork Chops

Preparation Time: 5 minutes

Cooking Time: 6 hours

Servings: 8

Ingredients:

- 2 pounds pasture-raised pork chops

- 1 teaspoon salt

- 1 tablespoon dried thyme

- 1 tablespoon dried rosemary

- 1 tablespoon ground cumin

- 1 tablespoon dried curry powder

- 1 tablespoon chopped fresh chives

- 1 tablespoon fennel seeds

- 1 tablespoons avocado oil

Directions:

1   Place 2 tablespoons oil in a small bowl, add remaining ingredients except for pork, and stir until well mixed.

2   Rub this mixture on all sides of pork chops until evenly coated.

3   Grease a 6-quart slow cooker with remaining oil, add seasoned pork chops, and shut with lid.

4   Plug in the slow cooker and cook pork for 6 hours at a low heat setting or 4 hours at a high heat setting.

5   Serve straight away.

Nutrition:

Net Carbs: 1g

Calories: 235

Total Fat: 15g

Saturated Fat: 3g

Protein: 24g

Carbs: 1g

Fiber: 0g

Sugar: 0g

Spicy Pork & Spinach Stew

Preparation Time: 5 minutes

Cooking Time: 4 hours and 20 minutes

Servings: 5

Ingredients:

- 1-pound pasture-raised pork butt, fat trimmed and cut into 2-inch pieces

- 4 cups chopped baby spinach

- 4 ounces Rotel tomatoes

- 1 large white onion, peeled and quartered

- cloves of garlic, peeled

- 1 teaspoon dried thyme

- 2 teaspoons Cajun seasoning blend

- 2 tablespoons avocado oil

- ¾ cup heavy whipping cream

Directions:

1   Place tomatoes, onion, and garlic in a food processor and pulse for 1 to 2 minutes or until blended.

2   Pour this mixture into a 6-quart slow cooker, add Cajun seasoning mix, thyme, avocado oil, and pork pieces, and stir well until evenly coated.

3   Plug in the slow cooker, then shut with lid and cook for 5 hours at low heat setting or 2 hours at high heat setting.

4   When done, stir in cream until combined, add spinach and continue cooking at low heat setting for 20 minutes or more until spinach wilts.

5   Serve straight away.

Nutrition:

Net Carbs: 3.3g

Calories: 604

Total Fat: 38.3g

Saturated Fat: 9g

Protein: 56g

Carbs: 9g

Fiber: 5g;

Sugar: 4g

Stuffed Taco Peppers

Preparation Time: 5 minutes

Cooking Time: 8 hours

Servings: 6

Ingredients:

- 1 cup cauliflower rice

- 1 small red bell peppers

- 18-ounce minced pork, pasture-raised

- 1 teaspoon garlic powder

- ¾ teaspoon salt

- 1 teaspoon red chili powder

- 1 cup shredded Monterey jack cheese and more for topping

- 2 tablespoons avocado oil

- 1 cup water

Directions:

1   Remove and discard stem from each pepper and then scoop out seeds.

2   Place meat in a large bowl, add garlic, salt, and red chili powder, and stir until combined.

3   Then stir in cauliflower rice and oil until just combine and then stir in cheese.

4   Stuff this mixture into each pepper and place them in a 4-quart slow cooker.

5   Pour water into the bottom of the slow cooker, switch it on, and shut with the lid.

6   Cook peppers for 4 hours at high heat setting or 8 hours at low heating setting and top peppers with more cheese in the last 10 minutes of cooking time.

7   Serve straight away.

Nutrition:

Net Carbs: 4g

Calories: 270

Total Fat: 18g

Saturated Fat: 5g

Protein: 21g

Carbs: 6g

Fiber: 2g

Sugar: 3g

Chinese Pulled Pork

Preparation Time: 5 minutes

Cooking Time: 7 hours and 30 minutes

Servings: 6

Ingredients:

- 2.2-pound pasture-raised pork shoulder, fat trimmed

- 2 tablespoons garlic paste

- 2 teaspoons ginger paste

- 1 teaspoon smoked paprika

- drops Erythritol sweetener

- 1 tablespoons soy sauce

- 1 tablespoon tomato paste

- tablespoons tomato sauce, sugar-free

- 1 cup chicken broth

Directions:

1   Place pork in a 6-quart slow cooker.

2   Whisk together remaining ingredients until smooth and then pour over the pork.

3   Plug in the slow cooker, then shut with lid and cook for 7 hours at low heat setting or until pork is tender.

4   Then shred pork with two forks and stir well until evenly coated with sauce.

5   Continue cooking pork for 30 minutes or more at a low heating setting until sauce is thickened to desired consistency.

6   Serve straight away.

Nutrition:

Net Carbs: 2g

Calories: 447

Total Fat: 35g

Saturated Fat: 13g

Protein: 30g

Carbs: 3g

Fiber: 1g

Sugar: 2g

Bacon Wrapped Pork Loin

Preparation Time: 5 minutes

Cooking Time: 7 hours

Servings: 4

Ingredients:

- 2-pound pasture-raised pork loin roast, fat-trimmed

- strips of bacon, uncooked

- tablespoon dried onion soup mix, organic

- 1/4 cup water

Directions:

1   Pour water into a 6-quart slow cooker.

2   Rub seasoning mix on all sides of pork, then wrap with bacon and place into the slow cooker.

3   Plug in the slow cooker and cook for 7 hours at a low heat setting or 5 hours at a high heat setting.

4   Serve straight away.

Nutrition:

Net Carbs: 0g

Calories: 639

Total Fat: 41g

Saturated Fat: 19g

Protein: 69g

Carbs: 0g

Fiber: 0g

Sugar: 0g

Main

Keto Lasagna

Preparation time: 20 minutes

Cooking time: 7 hours

Servings: 6

Ingredients:

- oz ground beef

- 1 tablespoon tomato puree

- 1 zucchini

- oz Parmesan, grated

- 1 tablespoon butter

- ½ teaspoon salt

- 1 teaspoon paprika

- 1 teaspoon chili flakes

- 1 tablespoon full-fat heavy cream

Directions

1 Slice the zucchini lengthwise.

2 Mix the ground beef, salt, paprika, and chili flakes.

3 Then mix the full-fat cream and tomato puree.

4 Chop the butter and put it in the slow cooker.

5 Make a layer of the zucchini in the bottom of the slow cooker bowl.

6 Put a layer of the ground beef mixture on top of the zucchini layer.

7 After this repeat, the same layers until you use all the ingredients.

8 Sprinkle the lasagna with the grated Parmesan and close the lid.

9 Cook the lasagna for 7 hours on Low.

10 Chill the cooked meal and serve!

Nutrition:

calories 197,

fat 11,

fiber 0.5,

carbs 2.5, protein 22.5

Butter Chicken

Preparation time: 15 minutes

Cooking time: 3 hours

Servings: 4

Ingredients:

- 1 tablespoons butter

- oz spinach, chopped

- 1 teaspoon onion powder

- 1 teaspoon paprika

- oz chicken breast, skinless, boneless

- ½ teaspoon salt

- ¼ cup chicken stock

Directions:

1   Beat the chicken breasts gently to tenderize and sprinkle it with the salt and paprika.

2   Then place the butter and spinach in a blender.

3   Add onion powder and blend the mixture for 1 minute at high speed.

4   Spread the chicken breast with the butter mixture on each side.

5   Place the buttered chicken in the slow cooker and the chicken stock.

6   Close the lid and cook the chicken for 3 hours on Low.

7   Serve the chicken immediately!

Nutrition:

calories 208,

fat 13.9,

fiber 0.7,

carbs 1.6,

protein 18.9

Tuscan Chicken

Preparation time: 15 minutes

Cooking time: 7 hours

Servings: 8

Ingredients:

- 1-pound chicken breast, skinless, boneless

- 1 tablespoon olive oil

- ½ cup full-fat cream

- 1 oz spinach, chopped

- oz Parmesan, grated

- 1 teaspoon chili flakes

- ½ teaspoon paprika

- 1 teaspoon minced garlic

- ½ teaspoon ground black pepper

Directions:

1 Chop the chicken breast roughly and sprinkle it with the chili flakes, paprika, minced garlic, and ground black pepper.

2 Stir the chicken and transfer to the slow cooker.

3 Add the full-fat cream and olive oil.

4 Add spinach and grated cheese.

5 Stir the chicken gently and close the lid.

6 Cook the chicken for 7 hours on Low.

7 Transfer cooked Tuscan chicken on the serving plates and serve!

Nutrition:

calories 136,

fat 7.2,

fiber 0.2,

carbs 1.4, protein 16

Corned Beef

Preparation time: 10 minutes

Cooking time: 8 hours

Servings: 6

Ingredients:

- 1-pound corned beef

- 1 teaspoon peppercorns

- 1 teaspoon chili flakes

- 1 teaspoon mustard seeds

- 1 bay leaf

- 1 teaspoon salt

- 1 oz bacon fat

- garlic cloves

- 1 cup water

- 1 tablespoon butter

Directions:

1   Mix the peppercorns, chili flakes, mustard seeds, and salt in the bowl.

2   Then rub the corned beef with the spice mixture well.

3   Peel the garlic and place it in the slow cooker.

4   Add the corned beef.

5   Add water, butter, and bay leaf.

6   Add the bacon fat and close the lid.

7   Cook the corned beef for 8 hours on Low.

8   When the corned beef is cooked, discard the bay leaf, then transfer the beef to a plate and cut into servings.

9   Enjoy!

Nutrition:

calories 178,

fat 13.5,

fiber 0.3,

carbs 1.3,

protein 12.2

Sardine Pate

Preparation time: 15 minutes

Cooking time: 3 hours

Servings: 6

Ingredients:

- ½ cup water

- 1 tablespoons butter

- 1 teaspoon onion powder

- 1 teaspoon dried parsley

- oz sardine fillets, chopped

Directions:

1 Put the chopped sardine fillets, dried parsley, onion powder, and water in the slow cooker.

2 Close the lid and cook the fish for 3 hours on Low.

3 Strain the sardine fillet and put it in a blender.

4 Add butter and blend the mixture for 3 minutes at high speed.

5 Transfer the cooked pate into serving bowls and serve!

Nutrition:

calories 170,

fat 12.3,

fiber 0, carbs 0.3,

protein 14.1

Spare Ribs

Preparation time: 10 minutes

Cooking time: 8 hours

Servings: 6

Ingredients:

- 1-pound pork loin ribs

- 1 teaspoon olive oil

- 1 teaspoon minced garlic

- ¼ teaspoon cumin

- ¼ teaspoon chili powder

- 1 tablespoon butter

- 1 tablespoons water

Directions:

1 Mix the olive oil, minced garlic, cumin, and chili flakes in a bowl.

2 Melt the butter and add to the spice mixture.

3 Stir it well and add water. Stir again.

4 Then rub the pork ribs with the spice mixture generously and place the ribs in the slow cooker.

5 Close the lid and cook the ribs for 8 hours on Low.

6 When the ribs are cooked, serve them immediately!

Nutrition:

calories 203,

fat 14.1, fiber 0.6,

carbs 10,

protein 9.8

Soup and Stew

Chicken and Noodles Soup

Preparation time: 10 minutes

Cooking time: 7 hours

Servings: 8

Ingredients:

- 1-pound chicken breast, skinless, boneless, chopped

- 1 teaspoon salt

- 1 teaspoon chili flakes

- 1 teaspoon coriander

- 1 cup bell pepper, chopped

- oz. egg noodles

- cups chicken stock

Directions:

1   Mix chicken breast with salt, chili flakes, coriander, and place in the slow cooker.

2   Add chicken stock and close the lid.

3   Cook the ingredients on Low for 6 hours.

4   Then add egg noodles and bell pepper and cook the soup for 1 hour on High.

Nutrition:

99 calories,

13.5g protein,

5.4g carbohydrates,

2.3g fat,

0.4g fiber,

40mg cholesterol,

1084mg sodium,

259mg potassium

Light Zucchini Soup

Preparation time: 15 minutes

Cooking time: 30 minutes

Servings: 4

Ingredients:

- 1 large zucchini

- 1 white onion, diced

- 2 cups beef broth

- 1 teaspoon dried thyme

- ½ teaspoon dried rosemary

Directions

1 Pour the beef broth into the slow cooker.

2 Add onion, dried thyme, and dried rosemary.

3 After this, make the spirals from the zucchini with the help of the paralyzer and transfer them to the slow cooker.

4 Close the lid and cook the soul on High for 30 minutes.

Nutrition:

64 calories,

6.2g protein,

6.5g carbohydrates,

1.6g fat,

1.6g fiber,

0mg cholesterol,

773mg sodium,

462mg potassium.

Garlic Bean Soup

Preparation time: 10 minutes

Cooking time: 8 hours

Servings: 4

Ingredients:

- 1 teaspoon minced garlic

- 1 cup celery stalk, chopped

- 1 cup white beans, soaked

- 2 cups water

- 1 teaspoon salt

- 1 teaspoon ground paprika

- 1 tablespoon tomato paste

Directions

1   Put all ingredients in the slow cooker and carefully stir until tomato paste is dissolved.

2   Then close the lid and cook the soup on low for 8 hours.

Nutrition:

178 calories,

12.3g protein,

2.5g carbohydrates,

0.6g fat,

8.5g fiber,

0mg cholesterol,

623mg sodium,

1031mg potassium.

Vegetables

Cauliflower Rice

Preparation time: 10 minutes

Cooking time: 2 hours

Servings: 6

Ingredients:

- 2 cups cauliflower, shredded

- 1 cup vegetable stock

- 1 cup of water

- 1 tablespoon cream cheese

- 1 teaspoon dried oregano

Directions

1 Put all ingredients in the slow cooker.

2 Close the lid and cook the cauliflower rice on High for 2 hours.

Nutrition

25 calories,

0.8g protein,

3.9g carbohydrates,

0.8g fat,

1.8g fiber,

2mg cholesterol,

153mg sodium,

211mg potassium

Squash Noodles

Preparation time: 15 minutes

Cooking time: 4 hours

Servings: 4

Ingredients:

- 1-pound butternut squash, seeded, halved

- 1 tablespoon vegan butter

- 1 teaspoon salt

- ½ teaspoon garlic powder

- 1 cup water

Directions

1   Pour water into the slow cooker.

2   Add butternut squash and close the lid.

3   Cook the vegetable on high for 4 hours.

4   Then drain water and shred the squash flesh with the help of the fork, and transfer in the bowl.

5   Add garlic powder, salt, and butter. Mix the squash noodles.

Nutrition

78 calories,

1.2g protein,

13.5g carbohydrates,

3g fat,

2.3g fiber,

8mg cholesterol,

612mg sodium,

406mg potassium

Thyme Tomatoes

Preparation time: 10 minutes

Cooking time: 5 hours

Servings: 4

Ingredients:

- 1-pound tomatoes, sliced

- 1 tablespoon dried thyme

- 1 teaspoon salt

- 1 tablespoons olive oil

- 1 tablespoon apple cider vinegar

- ½ cup of water

Directions

1   Put all ingredients in the slow cooker and close the lid.

2   Cook the tomatoes on Low for 5 hours.

Nutrition

83 calories,

1.1g protein,

4.9g carbohydrates,

7.3g fat,

1.6g fiber,

0mg cholesterol,

588mg sodium,

277mg potassium

Poultry and Chicken

Lemon Chicken Thighs

Preparation time: 10 minutes

Cooking time: 7 hours

Servings: 4

Ingredients:

- chicken thighs, skinless, boneless

- 1 lemon, sliced

- 1 teaspoon ground black pepper

- ½ teaspoon ground nutmeg

- 1 teaspoon olive oil

- 1 cup of water

Directions

1. Rub the chicken thighs with ground black pepper, nutmeg, and olive oil.

2. Then transfer the chicken to the slow cooker.

3. Add lemon and water.

4. Close the lid and cook the meal on LOW for 7 hours.

Nutrition

294 calories,

42.5g protein,

1.8g carbohydrates,

12.2g fat,

0.6g fiber,

130mg cholesterol,

128mg sodium,

383mg potassium.

Chicken Bowl

Preparation time: 15 minutes

Cooking time: 4 hours

Servings: 6

Ingredients:

- 1-pound chicken breast, skinless, boneless, chopped

- 1 cup sweet corn, frozen

- 1 teaspoon ground paprika

- 1 teaspoon onion powder

- 1 cup tomatoes, chopped

- 1 cup of water

- 1 teaspoon olive oil

Directions

1   Mix chopped chicken breast with ground paprika and onion powder. Transfer it to the slow cooker.

2   Add water and sweet corn. Cook the mixture on High for 4 hours.

3   Then drain the liquid and transfer the mixture in the bowl.

4   Add tomatoes and olive oil. Mix the meal.

Nutrition

122 calories,

17.2g protein,

6.3g carbohydrates,

3g fat,

1.1g fiber,

48mg cholesterol,

45mg sodium,

424mg potassium.

Snacks

Spicy Pecans

Preparation Time: 10 minutes

Cooking Time: 3 hours

Servings: 16

Ingredients:

- lbs. pecan halves

- tbsp. Cajun seasoning blend

- tbsp. olive oil

Directions:

1 Add all ingredients to the slow cooker and stir well to combine.

2 Cover slow cooker with lid and cook on low for 1 hour.

3 Stir well. Cover again and cook for 2 hours more.

4 Serve and enjoy.

Nutrition:

Calories 607

Fat 62.5 g

Carbohydrates 12.2 g

Sugar 3 g

Protein 9.1 g

Cholesterol 0 mg

Tasty Seasoned Mixed Nuts

Preparation Time: 10 minutes

Cooking Time: 2 hours

Servings: 20

Ingredients:

- cups mixed nuts

- tbsp. curry powder

- tbsp. butter, melted

- Salt

Directions:

1   Add all ingredients into the slow cooker and stir well to combine.

2   Cover slow cooker with lid and cook on high for a ½ hour. Stir again and cook for 30 minutes more.

3   Cover again and cook on low for 1 hour more.

4   Stir well and serve.

Nutrition:

Calories 375

Fat 34.7 g

Carbohydrates 12.8 g

Sugar 2.5 g

Protein 9 g

Cholesterol 6 mg

Nacho Cheese Dip

Preparation Time: 10 minutes

Cooking Time: 2 hours

Servings: 8

Ingredients:

- oz. cream cheese, cut into chunks

- ¼ cup almond milk

- ½ cup chunky salsa

- 1 cup cheddar cheese, shredded

Directions:

1   Add all ingredients to the slow cooker and stir well.

2   Cover slow cooker with lid and cook on low for 2 hours. Stir to mix.

3   Serve with fresh vegetables.

Nutrition:

Calories 178

Fat 16.4 g

Carbohydrates 2.4 g

Sugar 0.9 g

Protein 6.1 g

Cholesterol 46 mg

Desserts

Apple, Avocado, and Mango Bowls

Preparation time: 10 minutes

Cooking time: 2 hours

Servings: 2

Ingredients:

- 1 cup avocado, peeled, pitted, and cubed

- 1 cup mango, peeled and cubed

- 1 apple, cored and cubed

- 2 tablespoons brown sugar

- 1 cup heavy cream

- 1 tablespoon lemon juice

Directions:

1. In your slow cooker, combine the avocado with the mango and the other ingredients, toss gently, put the lid on and cook on Low for 2 hours.

2   Divide the mix into bowls and serve.

Nutrition

Calories 60,

Fat 1,

Fiber 2,

Carbs 20, Protein 1

Ricotta Cream

Preparation time: 2 hours and 10 minutes

Cooking time: 1 hour

Servings: 10

Ingredients:

- ½ cup hot coffee

- 2 cups ricotta cheese

- ½ teaspoons gelatin

- 1 teaspoon vanilla extract

- 1 teaspoon espresso powder

- 1 teaspoon sugar

- 1 cup whipping cream

Directions:

1   In a bowl, mix coffee with gelatin, stir well and leave aside until coffee is cold.

2   In your slow cooker, mix espresso, sugar, vanilla extract, and ricotta and stir.

3   Add coffee mix and whipping cream, cover, cook on Low for 1 hour.

4   Divide into dessert bowls and keep in the fridge for 2 hours before serving.

Nutrition

Calories 200,

Fat 13,

Fiber 0,

Carbs 5,

Protein 7

Tomato Jam

Preparation time: 10 minutes

Cooking time: 3 hours

Servings: 2

Ingredients

- ½ pound tomatoes, chopped

- 1 green apple, grated

- 2 tablespoons red wine vinegar

- 2 tablespoons sugar

Directions:

- In your slow cooker, mix the tomatoes with the apple with the other ingredients, put the lid on, and cook on Low for 3 hours.

- Whisk the jam well, blend a bit using an immersion blender, divide into bowls and serve cold.

Nutrition

Calories 70,

Fat 1,

Fiber 1,

Carbs 18,

Protein 1

Green Tea Pudding

Preparation time: 10 minutes

Cooking time: 1 hour

Servings: 2

Ingredients:

- ½ cup coconut milk

- 1 and ½ cup avocado, pitted and peeled

- 2 tablespoons green tea powder

- 2 teaspoons lime zest, grated

- 1 tablespoon sugar

Directions:

1   In your slow cooker, mix coconut milk with avocado, tea powder, lime zest, and sugar, stir, cover, and cook on Low for 1 hour.

2   Divide into cups and serve cold.

Nutrition

Calories 107,

Fat 5,

Fiber 3,

Carbs 6,
Protein 8

Conclusion

Thank you for reading to the end of the Slow Cooker Keto Cookbook. We hope it was informative and provided you with all the tools you need to achieve your goals, whatever they may be.

As you go along, as you now know, so many new ways to cook your food, just decide which one you want to make first for your family and friends. Make a list of all the ingredients needed to prepare the different meals. Each of the provided recipes has provided the nutritional factors you need to prepare a healthy meal. You will learn how easy it is to prepare these meals. It will be much easier to calculate the carbohydrates you eat on a daily basis.

Here are some tips to keep you on track when on the ketogenic diet:

• Reheat tasty leftovers.

• Eat low-carb snacks.

• Drink coffee or tea instead of something sweet.

Anyone can make mistakes. Here are a few to keep in mind when using your keto recipes to get healthier:

• Maintain discipline. All you have to do is stay determined with your goals by moving from regular to ketogenic meals.

• Listen to your body. Your body knows more than you think because it understands how many servings of food you need to maintain your exercise routine. If you are hungry, eat; if you are not hungry, do not eat.

• Don't look for shortcuts. Try to plan your meals in advance so as not to eat carbohydrates that are wasted on junk food. Save carbohydrates for food as a special treat. Resist the urge to eat that bag of chips. Instead, why not eat some tasty fruit?

• Do not go out. It will take more than a few days to get your plan in place. Follow the guidelines provided in this book because they are all calculated based on the carbohydrates, fats, and proteins your body needs.

• To plan. If you know that you will have a very busy schedule in the coming days, why not prepare some meals ahead of time and put them in the freezer?

There are three main components that make up a slow cooker, these are the outer shell, the inner food container, and a lid. The outer shell is constructed of metal and contains all the heating coils required for cooking the food, but the coils are built into the outer shell, so they are fully protected. The inner container is referred to as the crock, and this is constructed using ceramic that is glazed, and this fits snugly within the container. There are slow cookers where you can remove the inside container, ideal for when it comes to cleaning it! The final part of the slow cooker is the lid that is designed to fit perfectly to ensure none of the steam can escape during the cooking process.

The slow cooker cooks by combining the wattage and time. When you turn on your slow cooker, the coil heats up and transfers the heat from the outer shell to the space which is between the outer shell and crock, the base wall of the stoneware crock. This type of heat warms the pot to somewhere in between 180 – 300 degrees Fahrenheit (80 – 145 degrees Celsius.) This way of heat transferal cooks the ingredients gently, and they simmer gently on a low-temperature setting until the food is cooked perfectly.

CPSIA information can be obtained
at www.ICGtesting.com
Printed in the USA
BVHW051111260421
605873BV00019B/2375

9 781802 667776